INDIAN PRAIRIE PUBLIC LIBRARY DISTRICT

3 1946 00534 5795

DEC 1 9 2012

D1060420

EXTREME ANIMALS

REMARKABLE REPTILES

Isabel Thomas

INDIAN PRAIRIE PUBLIC LIBRARY
401 Plainfield Rd.
Darien, IL 60561

Chicago, Illinois

www.capstonepub.com
Visit our website to find out more information about Heinemann-Raintree books.

To order:
☎ Phone 800-747-4992
🖥 Visit www.capstonepub.com to browse our catalog and order online.

© 2013 Raintree
an imprint of Capstone Global Library, LLC
Chicago, Illinois

All rights reserved. No part of this publication may be reproduced or transmitted in any form or by any means, electronic or mechanical, including photocopying, recording, taping, or any information storage and retrieval system, without permission in writing from the publisher.

Edited by Daniel Nunn, John-Paul Wilkins, and Rebecca Rissman
Designed by Philippa Jenkins
Picture research by Elizabeth Alexander
Production by Victoria Fitzgerald

Originated by Capstone Global Library
Printed and bound in China by CTPS

16 15 14 13 12
10 9 8 7 6 5 4 3 2 1

Library of Congress Cataloging-in-Publication Data

Cataloging-in-Publication data is on file at the Library of Congress.

ISBN:
978-1-4109-4682-9 (HC) 978-1-4109-4688-1 (PB)

Acknowledgments
We would like to thank the following for permission to reproduce photographs: Alamy pp. 10 (© Dmitry Kobeza), 19 (© Scubazoo); Corbis pp. 8 (© Michael & Patricia Fogden), 11 (© Martin Harvey; Gallo Images), 15 (© Dave Watts/Visuals Unlimited); FLPA pp. 12 (Fabio Pupin), 27 (Mark Moffett/Minden Pictures); Getty Images p. 24 (Mark Deeble and Victoria Stone/OSF); Nature Picture Library p. 13 (© Bence Mate); NHPA p. 16 (Stephen Dalton); Photolibrary pp. 5 (Nick Garbutt/OSF), 6 (Gunter Ziesler/Peter Arnold Images), 7 (Berndt Fischer/Age fotostock), 9 (Ed Reschke/Peter Arnold Images), 14 (Raymond Mendez/Animals Animals), 17 (Nick Garbutt/OSF), 18 (Oxford Scientific), 20 (Wolfgang Kaehler/Superstock); Photoshot p. 21 (© NHPA); Shutterstock pp. 4 (© TessarTheTegu), 22 (© Ryan M. Bolton), 23 (© Summer), 25 (© Stanjoman), 26 (© Julian W).

Main cover photograph of chameleon reproduced with permission of Shutterstock (© infografick). Background cover photograph of snake skin pattern reproduced with permission of Shutterstock (© Sergej Razvodovskij).

Every effort has been made to contact copyright holders of material reproduced in this book. Any omissions will be rectified in subsequent printings if notice is given to the publisher.

Disclaimer
All the Internet addresses (URLs) given in this book were valid at the time of going to press. However, due to the dynamic nature of the Internet, some addresses may have changed, or sites may have changed or ceased to exist since publication. While the author and publisher regret any inconvenience this may cause readers, no responsibility for any such changes can be accepted by either the author or the publisher.

Some words are shown in bold, **like this**. You can find out what they mean by looking in the glossary.

Contents

Extreme Reptiles 4

Never Hug a Boa! 6

Sneaky Snakes. 8

Killer Crocs. 10

Experts at Escaping. 12

Cross-Eyed Chameleons. 16

Turtle Power 18

Komodo Dragons 20

Tough Tortoises. 22

Awful Alligators 24

Terrible Tuataras. 26

Record-Breakers. 28

Glossary. 30

Find Out More 31

Index 32

Extreme Reptiles

Do you think you know everything about reptiles? Think again! Most reptiles have scaly skin, and they cannot make their own body heat. But the differences between reptiles are what make them **extreme**.

This gecko's weird body shape helps him to hide.

Some reptiles have strange bodies. Some behave in weird ways. These features help them find **mates** or food— or avoid getting eaten themselves!

Never Hug a Boa!

Could you swallow a goat in one gulp? This is no problem for a boa. These huge snakes coil around their **prey** and squeeze it until it cannot breathe. Like all snakes, they swallow their meal whole.

One large meal will fill a boa up for six months.

DID YOU KNOW?
Anacondas are boas that live in water. They are the largest snakes in the world.

Sneaky Snakes

Small snakes make tasty snacks for **predators**. This coral snake does not need to hide from predators. Its bright colors warn that it has a deadly bite.

The hognose snake should win an acting award! If it gets attacked, it pretends to be dead. Its tongue hangs out. It even makes a disgusting smell like a dead animal.

Killer Crocs

Saltwater crocodiles are the largest reptiles in the world. They are powerful **predators**. Crocodiles have the strongest bite of any animal. Being caught in a croc's jaws would be like being trapped under a large car.

DID YOU KNOW?
Saltwater crocodiles can grow up to 23 feet long. That's about one-and-a-half times the length of a car!

11

Experts at Escaping

There are more than 4,500 types of lizards. Some have **extreme** tricks to avoid getting eaten. A gecko does not panic if a **predator** grabs its tail. It runs away and leaves its tail behind. Then it grows a new one!

new tail

DID YOU KNOW?
A basilisk lizard's feet move so fast, it can run across water!

13

Horned lizards **distract** enemies with a disgusting trick. They squirt blood from their eyes! They do this by bursting **blood vessels** around their eyelids. The jet of blood can travel more than 3 feet.

When an Australian frilled lizard is in danger, it opens its neck frill like an umbrella. This makes it seem bigger.

Cross-Eyed Chameleons

Chameleons are famous for changing color. One of the reasons they do this is to **camouflage**, or hide, themselves.

long, sticky tongue shoots out to grab **prey**

Chameleons have **extreme** eyes. They can point in different directions! They can look out for danger and dinner at the same time.

17

Turtle Power

When the alligator snapping turtle gets hungry, it sticks its weird tongue out. Fish think that the tongue is a wriggling worm. But it is a trap. When the fish come to take a bite, the turtle's jaws go "snap"!

tongue

DID YOU KNOW?

Leatherback turtles can hold their breath for more than one hour.

19

Komodo Dragons

These frightening **predators** are the heaviest lizards on Earth. They have jagged teeth like a shark and a **venomous** bite. Komodo dragons knock over big animals and then rip their **prey** to pieces.

venomous
spit

21

Tough Tortoises

Nothing can bite through the shell of a giant tortoise. This helps them to live for more than 100 years. One pet tortoise even lived to celebrate his 255th birthday!

DID YOU KNOW?

The giant tortoise has a flat nose that helps it to drink through its nostrils. This helps it to suck up water from very shallow pools.

Awful Alligators

Alligators look heavy and clumsy. But these reptiles can spin their bodies like ice skaters. The famous death roll helps alligators to tear **prey** into chunks. They bite their prey and then spin around really fast. They can rip off an arm or a leg in seconds.

powerful
tail

webbed
foot

Terrible Tuataras

Tuataras have three eyes! The third eye can only be seen when they are babies. No one knows what it is for. It may help young tuataras to avoid their parents. Adult tuataras will eat their own babies!

third eye hidden under skin

tail falls off if attacked

DID YOU KNOW?
Tuataras have been around since the time of the dinosaurs.

Record-Breakers

Which reptile do you think is the most **extreme**? Why? Take a look at some of these record-breaking reptiles to help you decide.

What? Chameleon

Why? Longest tongue

Wow! Some chameleons have tongues one-and-a-half times as long as their bodies!

What? Leatherback turtle

Why? World's heaviest reptile

Wow! The biggest turtle ever found weighed about 2,000 pounds. That is more than some cars!

What? Saltwater crocodile

Why? Largest reptile

Wow! Males can grow up to 23 feet long. But most are hunted by humans before they get this big.

What? Small-scaled snake

Why? Most **venomous** snake

Wow! These Australian snakes have enough venom (poison) to kill 100 adults!

What? Spiny-tailed iguana

Why? Fastest reptile on land

Wow! This reptile from Costa Rica can run at 22 miles per hour. That is about the same speed as an Olympic sprinter.

What? Dwarf gecko

Why? Smallest reptile

Wow! Dwarf geckos measure just over half an inch from the nose to the tip of the tail. That is not even as wide as a dime!

Glossary

blood vessel tube in an animal's body that blood moves through

camouflage colors or markings that help an animal to blend in with the things around it

distract draw somebody's attention away from something

extreme unusual, amazing, or different from normal

mate animal that can have babies together with another animal

predator animal that hunts other animals for food

prey animal that is hunted by another animal for food

saltwater living in salty water

venomous able to produce venom. Venomous animals have a poisonous bite or sting.

Find Out More

Books

Hibbert, Clare. *Snakes and Lizards* (Really Weird Animals). Mankato, Minn.: Arcturus, 2011.

Solway, Andrew. *Deadly Reptiles* (Wild Predators). Chicago: Heinemann Library, 2005.

Weber, Belinda. *Animal Disguises* (Discover Science). Boston: Kingfisher, 2007.

Woolf, Alex. *Killer Snakes* (Animal Attack). Mankato, Minn.: Arcturus, 2012.

Web sites

Learn more about snakes at this web site:
kids.discovery.com/tell-me/animals/reptiles/slitherin-snakes

Find facts, photos, and more about reptiles here:
nationalzoo.si.edu/Animals/ReptilesAmphibians/ForKids/default.cfm

Watch amazing videos of reptiles at this web site:
video.nationalgeographic.com/video/player/kids/animals-pets-kids/reptiles-kids/

Index

alligator snapping turtles 18

alligators 24–25

anacondas 7

Australian frilled lizards 15

basilisk lizards 13

boas 6–7

chameleons 16–17, 28

coral snakes 8

crocodiles 10–11, 29

death roll 24

drinking 23

dwarf geckos 29

geckos 5, 12, 29

giant tortoises 22–23

hognose snakes 9

horned lizards 14

iguanas 29

Komodo dragons 20–21

leatherback turtles 19, 28

lizards 12–15, 20–21

predators 8, 10, 12, 20

prey 6, 16, 18, 20, 24

saltwater crocodiles 10–11, 29

small-scaled snakes 29

snakes 6–9, 29

spiny-tailed iguanas 29

tails 12, 25, 26

tongues 9, 16, 18, 28

tuataras 26–27

turtles 18–19, 28

venomous reptiles 20, 21, 29